NOTE TO PARENTS

Welcome to Kingfisher Readers! This program is designed to help young readers build skills, confidence, and a love of reading as they explore their favorite topics.

These tips can help you get more from the experience of reading books together. But remember, the most important thing is to make reading fun!

Tips to Warm Up Before Reading

- Look through the book with your child. Ask them what they notice about the pictures.
- Wonder aloud together. Ask questions and make predictions. What will this book be about? What are some words we could expect to find on these pages?

While Reading

- Take turns or read together until your child takes over.
- Point to the words as you say them.
- When your child gets stuck on a word, ask if the picture could help. Then think about the first letter too.
- Accept and praise your child's contributions.

After Reading

- Look back at the things your child found interesting. Encourage connections to other things you both know.
- Draw pictures or make models to explore these ideas.
- Read the book again soon, to build fluency.

With five distinct levels and a wealth of appealing topics, the Kingfisher Readers series provides children with an exciting way to learn to read about the world around them. Enjoy!

Ellie Costa, M.S. Ed.
Literacy Specialist, Bank Street School for Children, New York

KINGFISHER
READERS

level
3

Ancient Rome

Philip Steele

KINGFISHER
NEW YORK

Copyright © Kingfisher 2012
Published in the United States by Kingfisher,
175 Fifth Ave., New York, NY 10010
Kingfisher is an imprint of Macmillan Children's Books, London.
All rights reserved.

Distributed in the U.S. and Canada by Macmillan,
175 Fifth Ave., New York, NY 10010

Library of Congress Cataloging-in-Publication data
has been applied for.

Series editor: Thea Feldman
Literacy consultant: Ellie Costa, Bank St. College, New York

ISBN: 978-0-7534-6903-3 (HB)
ISBN: 978-0-7534-6904-0 (PB)

Kingfisher books are available for special promotions
and premiums. For details contact: Special Markets
Department, Macmillan, 175 Fifth Ave., New York, NY 10010.

For more information, please visit
www.kingfisherbooks.com

Printed in China
9 8 7 6 5 4 3 2 1
1TR/0712/UG/WKT/105MA

Picture credits
The Publisher would like to thank the following for permission to reproduce their images
(t = top, b = bottom, c = center, r = right, l = left): Pages 4 Shutterstock/G2019; 5 Getty/Pierre Andrieu/AFP;
7b Corbis/Roger Ressmeyer; 10b Shutterstock/Sergielev; 11 Shutterstock/riekephotos; 13t Art Archive/
Archaeological Museum Alexandria/Dagli Orti; 15 Corbis/Massimo Borchi; 21t Art Archive/Musee de la
Civilisation Gallo-Romaine Lyon/Gianni Dagli Orti; 25 Shutterstock/Rui Vale de Sousa; 27 Art Archive/ Musee
Archaeologique Naples/Alfredo Dagli Orti; 28 Getty/Joseph Barrak/AFP; all other images Kingfisher artbank.

Contents

From city to empire

Rome is a major city in Italy. It is a very old city. It is more than 2,700 years old. Rome began small but grew in size and power. About one million people lived there. During ancient times, Rome was the biggest city in the world.

Rome grew from the world's largest city into an **empire**. Rome ruled many countries. The countries were **conquered** by the Roman army.

The Pont du Gard bridge in France was built during the time of the Roman Empire.

This beautiful floor in Bordeaux, France dates back to Roman times.

Uncovering the past

We learn about the past by studying things we find from long ago. An entire town from the time of the Roman Empire has been found! It is called Pompeii (say "Pom-PAY").

Vesuvius erupting

Pompeii is in Italy. It was buried under ash and rocks when the volcano Vesuvius erupted there in 79 CE. Thousands of people died. Hundreds of years later, ancient streets and buildings were found under the rocks. Many other things, such as pots, pans, and coins were found too.

CAVE CANEM

The **ruins** of Pompeii help us understand daily life during the Roman Empire. The photo below shows Pompeii today.

In the empire

Rome became an empire in 27 BCE. This
happened after a long **civil war**. Before
and after its civil war, Rome conquered
many other lands. The countries that are
today Spain, France, and Britain were
once part of the Roman Empire. Some
of Germany was too.

In an empire, an **emperor** is in charge. The
first Roman emperor was named Augustus.

The empire included Romania, Greece, western Asia, and northern Africa too. The empire covered a lot of land!

The founders of Rome

According to one old story, twin brothers named Romulus and Remus founded Rome. As babies, the brothers were left by a river. They were rescued and raised by a wolf!

Roads were built all over the empire.

Trading goods

Roman **traders** traveled far to buy and sell many goods. Pottery, cloth, olive oil, and wine were some goods. They were sold to the public in markets and shops at a meeting place called a **forum**. Every Roman city had a forum.

This Roman jar probably held wine or oil.

Roman coins

Romans traded goods for other goods or paid with coins. Roman coins were made of gold, silver, bronze, or copper. General Julius Caesar (say "See-zer") was the first Roman to have his face shown on a coin while he was still alive.

Pirate attack!
Many goods passed through **port** cities such as Ostia. In 68 BCE pirates attacked Ostia. The Romans fought back and won!

The Roman army

The Roman army was divided into large groups called **legions**. Each legion had around 5,000 soldiers. Roman soldiers wore heavy armor on top of their clothes.

They also wore helmets and carried shields. These things protected them from the enemies' weapons. The Romans fought using short swords, daggers, and spears.

A Roman soldier ready for battle

Julius Caesar won many battles for Rome. He later became the ruler of all Rome. But many people thought he had too much power. He was murdered in 44 BCE.

Julius Caesar

The tortoise
Roman soldiers sometimes marched close together, covered by their shields. They looked like a giant tortoise, with the shields forming a shell!

Roman gods

The Romans believed in many different gods. There was a god of the sea, a god of love, a god of war, and more. Jupiter was the king of all gods. He was also the god of the sky. People believed that if they were bad, Jupiter would throw a lightning bolt at them.

Jupiter

Juno

Diana

Mars

Neptune

Apollo

Venus

A temple in France

The Romans built temples to honor their gods. They held festivals for them there. There was food, music, and, sometimes, presents for the public!

The Pantheon
In 126 BCE, the Pantheon was built in Rome to honor all the gods. Pantheon is a Greek word that means "all gods."

15

Homes of ancient Rome

There were many kinds of homes. In big cities, such as Rome and Ostia, there were a lot of apartments.

In towns, many homes had an open **courtyard**. In the courtyard there were often pools of water. In the country, rich people owned big homes called villas. Some villas had **mosaics** made from tiles. The tiles were placed into the floor to form patterns or images of things such as animals.

The Romans believed that the gods protected their homes. They made **offerings** to them every day.

This was the home of one wealthy family!

Food and feasts

People in ancient Rome did not eat much for breakfast or lunch. Dinner was the main meal of the day.

In a rich home, cooks boiled food in pots and pans on a brick stove. They used many herbs and spices to flavor the food. Pork, fish, or chicken were main dishes. Vegetables included onions, peas, and cabbages. Figs and grapes were popular fruits.

Rich people sometimes held **banquets**. Guests at a banquet ate from a low table, using fingers and knives.

On the menu
Mice cooked in honey. Snails in wine. Dumplings filled with brains. Boiled ostrich. All were banquet foods!

Clothes

Everyone in ancient Rome wore **tunics**. Many women wore long tunics. Slaves, children, and those who did physical work wore short tunics.

A woman wore a woolen dress called a **stola** over her tunic. Many women did their hair in the latest styles and wore jewelry, makeup, and perfume.

Pretty poison
Roman women liked to look pale. They put chalk or white lead on their faces. But the lead had poison in it. It could make them sick!

Emerald and gold earrings from ancient Rome

The **toga** was an important piece of clothing worn by men. It was a heavy white robe that wrapped around the body. One end hung over one shoulder. Slaves were not allowed to wear togas.

In the arena

Ancient Romans gathered at **arenas** (say "uh-ree-nuhs") and theaters to watch events. These places were large, round, and open to the sky. Seats were made of stone.

A chariot race

Chariot racing was a major sport. Thousands of people gathered at an arena called Circus Maximus to watch the races.

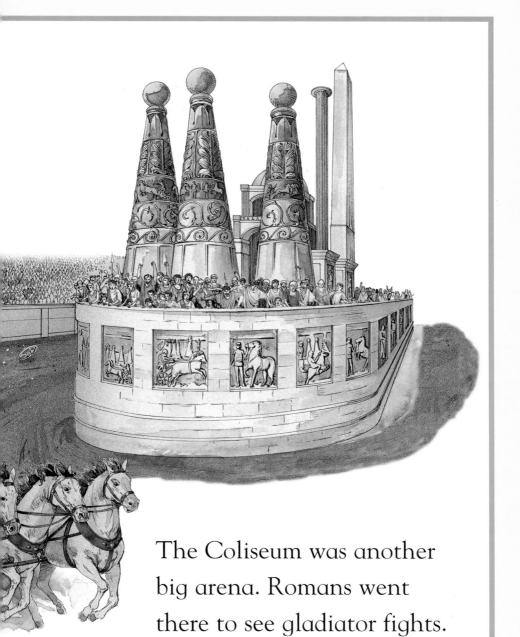

The Coliseum was another big arena. Romans went there to see gladiator fights. Gladiators were men trained to fight to the death!

Public baths

The public bathhouse was another popular place to gather. Every Roman town had one. Most Roman homes did not have a bath. People went to a bathhouse to wash. There were hot tubs, cold tubs, and steam rooms. There were separate times for men and women.

People went to the baths to see friends, exercise, or just to relax. Many people went every day.

Ancient baths in England

Getting clean
Romans did not use soap. They rubbed themselves with oil instead. Then they scraped themselves clean.

Education

Most families were not rich enough to send their children to school. So most children could not read or write.

Children who did go to school started at age seven. They each had a board covered with wax. They wrote on it with a pointed tool. They smoothed the wax over to use the board again. They learned to read, write, and do math.

Lucky charms

A newborn child was given a charm called a **bulla**. The charm was to keep the child safe. A girl wore the charm until she married. A boy wore it until he turned 16.

Some boys learned more. They learned history, poetry, and how to make speeches. Girls learned how to take care of a home. They learned to play musical instruments too.

The end of the empire

The Roman Empire became very large. It was divided into an eastern and western empire. Constantinople was the main city in the east. Rome remained the main city in the west.

The empire fought its enemies for hundreds of years. Finally, in the fifth century, people called Goths took over the city of Rome. That was the beginning of the end of the empire.

We still find ruins from ancient Rome today.

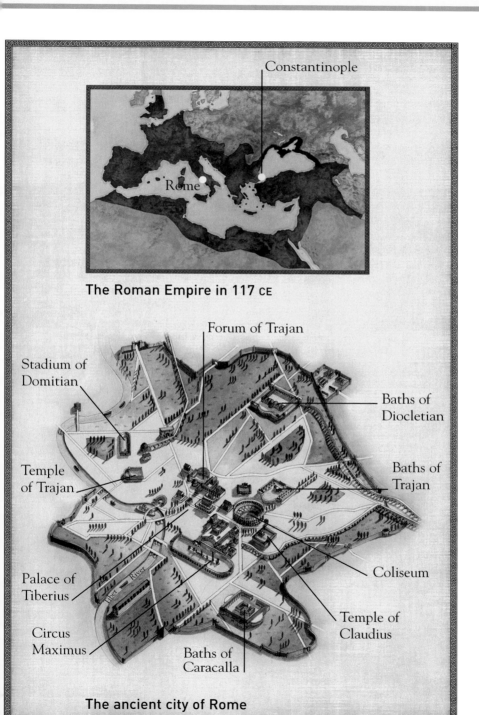

Constantinople

Rome

The Roman Empire in 117 CE

Forum of Trajan

Stadium of
Domitian

Baths of
Diocletian

Temple
of Trajan

Baths of
Trajan

Palace of
Tiberius

Coliseum

Tiber River

Circus
Maximus

Temple of
Claudius

Baths of
Caracalla

The ancient city of Rome

29

Glossary

arenas large places with seats where people watch events

banquets big feasts with guests

bulla a charm given to newborns to keep them safe

chariot a small cart pulled by a horse

civil war a war between people in the same country

conquered took control by force

courtyard an outdoor area inside a large building

empire several countries under the rule of one ruler or country

emperor a man who rules an empire

forum a public meeting place in an ancient Roman town

legions large groups of soldiers in the ancient Roman army

mosaics patterns or images formed by tiles set in the floor

offerings something given to honor or please a god

port a town by water where boats can load and unload goods

ruins what is left of very old things

stola a dress worn by an ancient Roman woman over a tunic

toga a white robe worn by important men in Rome

traders people who buy and sell things

tunics common items of clothing worn in ancient Rome—a tunic could be long or short, depending on who was wearing it

Index

If you have enjoyed reading this book, look out for more in the Kingfisher Readers series!

KINGFISHER READERS: LEVEL 1

Baby Animals
Busy as a Bee
Butterflies
Colorful Coral Reefs
Jobs People Do
Seasons
Snakes Alive!
Trains

KINGFISHER READERS: LEVEL 2

What Animals Eat
Where Animals Live
Where We Live
Your Body

KINGFISHER READERS: LEVEL 3

Ancient Rome
Dinosaur World
Record Breakers—The Biggest
Volcanoes

KINGFISHER READERS: LEVEL 4

Flight
Pirates
Sharks
Weather

KINGFISHER READERS: LEVEL 5

Ancient Egyptians
Rainforests
Record Breakers—The Fastest
Space

For guidance for teachers and parents and activities and fun stuff for
kids, go to the Kingfisher Readers website:
www.kingfisherreaders.com